TORNADOES

BILL McAULIFFE

CREATIVE EDUCATION · CREATIVE PAPERBACKS

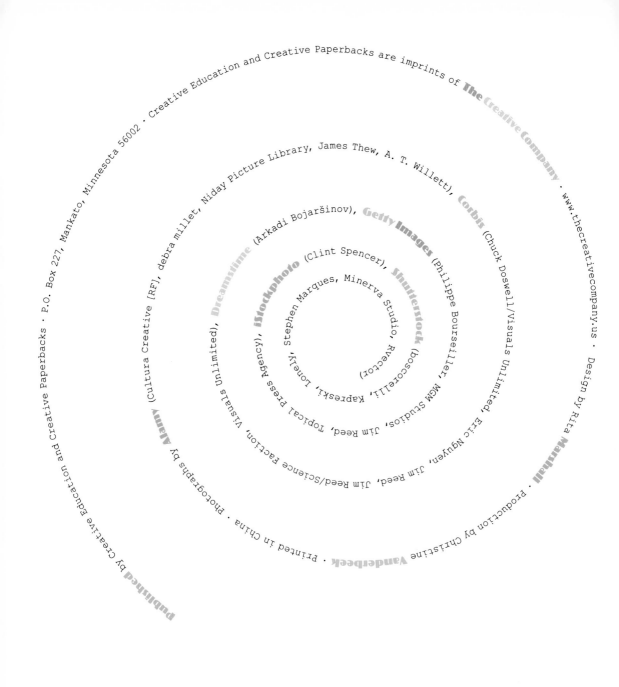

Published by Creative Education and Creative Paperbacks • P.O. Box 227, Mankato, Minnesota 56002 • Creative Education and Creative Paperbacks are imprints of The Creative Company • www.thecreativecompany.us • Design by Rita Marshall • Production by Christine Vanderbeek • Printed in China • Photographs by Alamy (Cultura Creative [RF], debra millet, Niday Picture Library, James Thew, A. T. Willett), Corbis (Chuck Doswell/Visuals Unlimited, Eric Nguyen, Jim Reed, Topical Press Agency, Visuals Unlimited), Dreamstime (Arkadi Bojaršinov), Getty Images (Philippe Bourseiller, MGM Studios, Jim Reed, Jim Reed/Science Faction), iStockphoto (Clint Spencer), Shutterstock (bosorelli), Stephen Marques, Minerva Studio, Rvector), Kapreski, Lonely

Library of Congress Cataloging-in-Publication Data • Names: McAuliffe, Bill, author. • Title: Tornadoes / Bill McAuliffe. • Series: X-Books: Weather. • Includes bibliographical references and index. Summary: A countdown of five of the most devastating tornadoes provides thrills as readers discover more about the features of this whirling, funnel-shaped weather phenomenon. • IDENTIFIERS: LCCN 2016059691 / ISBN 978-1-60818-828-4 (HARDCOVER) / ISBN 978-1-62832-431-0 (PBK) / ISBN 978-1-56660-876-3 (EBOOK) Subjects: LCSH: Tornadoes—Juvenile literature. • CLASSIFICATION: LCC QC955.2.M375 2017 / DDC 551.55/3—DC23 CCSS: RI.3.1-8; RI.4.1-5, 7; RI.5.1-3, 8; RI.6.1-2, 4, 7; RH.6-8.3-8 First Edition HC 9 8 7 6 5 4 3 2 1 • First Edition PBK 9 8 7 6 5 4 3 2 1

TORNADOES

CONTENTS

WEATHER
BOOKS

FLYING DEBRIS

RUINED CROPS

LEVELED BUILDINGS

XTRAORDINARY WEATHER

Tornadoes are spinning columns of air. Their winds are powerful. They form quickly. And they are unpredictable. Tornadoes are the most destructive storms on Earth.

Tornado Basics

Tornadoes are formed by strong thunderstorms. They spin in a tight circle. Their winds can top 200 miles (322 km) per hour. They strip shingles off roofs and knock down power lines. They ruin crops in farmers' fields. Tornadoes can level an entire town. They can toss a railroad car. Some can even drive a piece of straw into a tree. Tornadoes carry debris for miles. This debris is dangerous. Flying at high speeds through the air, it can hurt or kill people.

AVERAGE NUMBER OF TORNADOES PER YEAR (1950–2015)

The United States began keeping an official count of tornadoes in 1950.

Washington
2

Montana
6

Oregon
2

Idaho
3

Wyoming
10

THE FIRST ACCURATE PREDICTION

of a tornado was made in 1948.

Nevada
1

California
6

Utah
2

Colorado
31

Alaska
0

Arizona
4

New Mexico
9

THE YEAR WITH THE FEWEST

tornado-related deaths

was 1986, with 15.

Hawaii
1

Nevada, Idaho, California, Alaska, and Hawaii

had never had a tornado-related death.

North Dakota
23

Minnesota
26

South Dakota
27

Wisconsin
20

Nebraska
42

Iowa
37

Michigan
15

Vermont
1

New Hampshire
1

Maine
2

New York
6

Massachusetts
3

Rhode Island
0

Connecticut
2

Kansas
61

Illinois
36

Indiana
21

Ohio
16

Pennsylvania
12

New Jersey
2

Delaware
1

Maryland
5

W. Virginia
2

Virginia
10

Missouri
33

Kentucky
14

Oklahoma
56

Arkansas
27

Tennessee
18

North Carolina
19

South Carolina
14

Mississippi
31

Alabama
30

Georgia
23

Texas
129

Louisiana
28

Florida
49

THE YEAR WITH THE MOST

tornado-related deaths

was 2011, with 553.

ONLY 16 STATES

have experienced more

than one EF5 tornado.

FORECASTING TORNADOES

Forecasters warn people about dangerous weather.

But they can tell only when a tornado *might* form.

They do not know exactly where a tornado will happen.

And they never know how strong it will be.

Tornadoes are difficult to study. A lot about them is still unknown. But forecasts are improving. Warnings are given earlier. Now people have more time to prepare. The areas warned are getting smaller, too. That means there are fewer false alarms.

Since the early 1990s, more tornadoes have been reported each year. This is in part due to better radar. But it is also because towns are growing. Tornadoes that may once have gone unreported are more likely to be seen.

Three out of four tornado warnings are false alarms.

FALSE ALARMS

TORNADO BASICS FACT

A tornado watch means conditions are right for a tornado to form.

A tornado warning means one has been spotted in the area.

Xtreme Tornado #5

The Wizard of Oz The most famous tornado in history may be one that was man-made. That was the tornado in the 1938 movie *The Wizard of Oz*. It was actually a 35-foot-long (10.7 m) stocking that was suspended from a crane and rotated with a motor. A powdery clay, carbon, and sulphur mix created the dark clouds and spinning dust at the base. The camera was rotated inside the sock to create Dorothy's view down the funnel.

Tornado Formation

About 2,000 thunderstorms are hitting Earth at all times. Any of them could produce a tornado. But a supercell thunderstorm is most likely to form a tornado. And only 2 of those 2,000 thunderstorms are supercells. Supercells are huge, rotating storms.

All thunderstorms are marked by an updraft of warm air. Updrafts can top 150 miles (241 km) per hour. Winds around an updraft may blow at different speeds or in different directions. That can cause the updraft to rotate.

A spinning updraft can form in other ways, too. Wind often blows along the ground. If the wind above it blows faster, it can curl into a tube. (This is similar to a breaking wave.) When this tube meets a storm's updraft, it can be tipped upward.

The spinning updraft can then become a mesocyclone. A mesocyclone is two to six miles (3.2–9.7 km) wide. High above the ground, it rotates within a supercell. As its spin tightens, a tornado can form.

Precipitation

clouds   thunderstorm

thunder, lightning

high winds, mesocyclone, funnel cloud

supercell   tornado

TORNADO FORMATION FACT

A funnel cloud is a rotating column of air that forms under a storm cloud. It is not a tornado until it touches the ground.

TOP FIVE XTREME TORNADOES

Xtreme Tornado #4

The Great St. Louis Tornado The downtown area of St. Louis, Missouri, has been hit by at least four tornadoes. The tornado that struck the city on May 27, 1896, is the third-deadliest in U.S. history. The tornado killed 137 in St. Louis. Across the Mississippi River in East St. Louis, Illinois, another 118 died. At the time, many poor people lived in houseboats on the river. Many were likely swept away and not included in the death count.

MAY 27, 1896

Since 1950, the number of U.S. deaths from tornadoes has averaged about 88 per year.

XCEPTIONAL TORNADOES

Tornadoes form year round. They occur all around the world. But the U.S. gets more than any other country. It is hit by about 1,225 tornadoes each year.

100% of Tornadoes

5%

75%   20%

in the U.S.

in Canada

in the rest of the world

TORNADO OCCURRENCES FACT

May is the most active tornado month in the U.S.

From 2000 to 2015, the month of May averaged 278 tornadoes per year.

The Midwest is known as Tornado Alley.

TORNADO X ALLEY

Tornado Occurrences

In the U.S., tornadoes are most common in the spring. The central plains provide the perfect conditions for thunderstorms to form. Warm, moist air from the Gulf of Mexico travels north. Cooler, dry air from the Rocky Mountains moves southeast. Over the flat land, warm and cool clash. Those violent meetings often create chains of thunderstorms. Hundreds of miles long, these storms are breeding grounds for tornadoes.

Tornadoes have occurred in every state. From 1950 to 2015, only four tornadoes were reported in Alaska. Rhode Island had the second-lowest tally with 11. Each year, Texas has more tornadoes than any other state. But Texas is huge. In terms of size, Florida is the most tornado-prone state. It is followed closely by Kansas.

XASPERATING STORMS

The average tornado warning time in the U.S. is 13 minutes. In that short span, people must make decisions that could mean life or death.

One of the deadliest tornado days in U.S. history was April 27, 2011. More than 315 people were killed as 207 tornadoes broke out.

XASPERATING STORMS FACT

From 1887 to the early 1950s, the word "tornado" was banned from forecasts. Government officials thought it would terrify people.

As buildings are
made stronger and
warnings improve,
the average number
of tornado deaths has
dropped. However, many
people ignore warnings.
Others simply do not know
how to stay safe in a tornado.
During a tornado, the safest
place is usually a basement. The
second best option is indoors,
low to the ground, and away from
windows. If there is time, people in
cars should move indoors—or at least
get out of their cars.
The U.S. had an unusual number of
twisters in 2011. It was hit by a record 1,692.
More than 550 people died. On May 22, 2011,
a tornado siren went off in Joplin, Missouri.
Residents had 17 minutes to prepare for the EF5
tornado. But 158 people died. It was the most deaths
from a single tornado since 1947. A weather service
study found that many people ignored the warning.

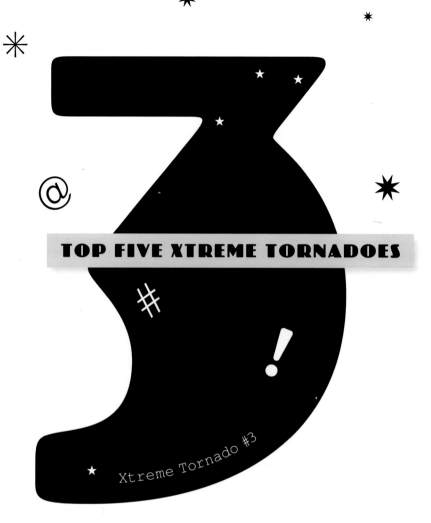

3

Xtreme Tornado #3

The Natchez Tornado Natchez, Mississippi, was a busy port on the Mississippi River in the 19th century. In 1840, a tornado struck the city. At least 317 people died. Of those killed, 269 worked on boats in the river. Sixty boats were destroyed. Though this is the second-deadliest U.S. tornado on record, there were probably more than 317 deaths. At the time, the death counts rarely included slaves.

MAY 6, 1840

XTENSIVE DESTRUCTION

Tornadoes are rated on the Enhanced Fujita scale. A tornado is not rated until after it falls apart. Rank is determined by damage.

Rating Tornadoes

Winds in a tornado are difficult to measure. Anemometers are almost always blown away. Instead, wind speed is estimated based on damages. The Enhanced Fujita, or EF, scale uses a list of buildings and damages. This list allows tornadoes to be rated consistently.

An EF0 tornado has the weakest winds. Its damages are usually light. EF5 tornadoes are the strongest. Their damages are described as incredible. An EF5 tornado can sweep away well-built houses. It can toss car-sized debris more than 109 yards (100 m). EF5 tornadoes are also quite rare. Typically, no more than one EF5 tornado a year touches down in the U.S. No matter how strong, whenever these spinning columns touch down, damage is almost guaranteed.

ENHANCED FUJITA SCALE

EF0	65–85 miles (105–137 km) per hour
EF1	86–110 miles (138–177 km) per hour
EF2	111–135 miles (178–217 km) per hour
EF3	136–165 miles (218–266 km) per hour
EF4	166–200 miles (267–322 km) per hour
EF5	greater than 200 miles (322 km) per hour

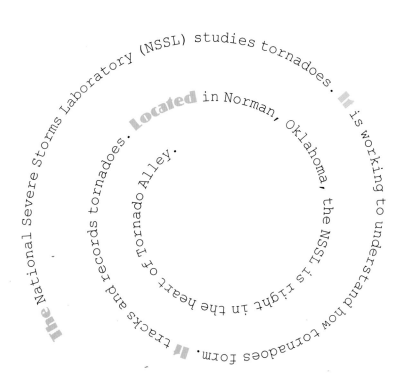

The National Severe Storms Laboratory (NSSL) studies tornadoes. It is working to understand how tornadoes form. It tracks and records tornadoes. Located in Norman, Oklahoma, the NSSL is right in the heart of Tornado Alley.

RATING TORNADOES FACT

On April 3, 1974, 147 tornadoes touched down in the U.S.

Seven of those were rated EF5. No other EF5 tornadoes formed that year.

Xtreme Tornado #2

The Tri-State Tornado is the deadliest tornado in American recorded history. It first touched down in Missouri. Then it crossed into Illinois. Finally, after traveling into Indiana, it disappeared. The tornado killed 695 people in total. Its path was a record 217 miles (349 km) long. The Tri-State also holds the U.S. record for time. It spent nearly three and a half hours on the ground.

MARCH 18, 1925

About 20 percent of supercell storms produce tornadoes.

Sometimes smaller satellite tornadoes develop and encircle a central tornado.

Most tornadoes travel about 35 miles (56.3 km) per hour.

Tornadoes do not form in very cold places, such as Antarctica.

The southeastern U.S. has more fatal tornadoes than any other part of the country.

From 1950 to 2015, the U.S. recorded 59 EF5 tornadoes.

In the 1800s, some people believed electrical forces from railroads and telegraph wires caused tornadoes.

Meteorologists sometimes spot the telltale hooked shape of a tornado on radar.

The widest tornado on record was 2.7 miles (4.3 km) across. It formed in El Reno, Oklahoma, on May 31, 2013.

Most tornadoes are 300 to 500 yards (274–457 m) wide.

The sounding of a second tornado siren does not mean "all clear." It means another one is on its way.

Tim Samaras, a leading tornado researcher, was killed by an Oklahoma twister in 2013.

Many people say tornadoes sound like freight trains.

As of 2015, Colorado's

Weld County had been hit by more tornadoes than any other U.S. county.

APRIL 26, 1989

Xtreme Tornado #1

Bangladesh Tornado The deadliest tornado
in recorded history occurred in Bangladesh
in 1989. It tore a path one mile (1.6 km)
wide. It traveled 10 miles (16.1 km)
along the ground. Many of the country's
buildings were poorly built. Two cities
were completely destroyed. No warnings
were issued. People did not have time
to reach safety. Bangladesh is densely
populated. About 1,300 people died.
Another 12,000 were hurt.

GLOSSARY

anemometers – devices that measure wind speed

mesocyclone – the broad, rotating area of a thunderstorm about five miles (8 km) above the ground

radar – technology that detects objects from a distance, as well as their speed and direction

RESOURCES

Bluestein, Howard B. *Tornado Alley: Monster Storms of the Great Plains*. New York: Oxford University Press, 1999.

Edwards, Roger. National Oceanic and Atmospheric Administration Storm Prediction Center. "The Online Tornado FAQ." http://www.spc.noaa.gov/faq/tornado/.

Farndon, John. *Extreme Weather*. New York: Dorling Kindersley, 2007.

Grazulis, Thomas P. *The Tornado: Nature's Ultimate Windstorm*. Norman: University of Oklahoma Press, 2001.

INDEX

Scientists believe that each tornado produces its own signature sound.